Lectures And Discourses - III

by

Swami Vivekananda

Lectures And Discourses - III
by Swami Vivekananda

ISBN: 978-93-59393-68-1

Published by

DOUBLE 9 BOOKS

2/13-B, Ansari Road
Daryaganj, New Delhi – 110002
info@double9books.com
www.double9books.com
Tel. 011-40042856

ABOUT THE AUTHOR

Swami Vivekananda was born Narendranath Datta in India on January 12, 1863. He died on July 4, 1902, and was the most important student of the Indian saint Ramakrishna. He was an important part of bringing Vedanta and Yoga to the West. He is also charged with making people more aware of other religions and making Hinduism a major world religion. Vivekananda had a lot of success at the Parliament. In the years that followed, he gave hundreds of lectures across the United States, England, and Europe to spread the main ideas of Hinduism. He also started the Vedanta Society of New York and the Vedanta Society of San Francisco, which is now the Vedanta Society of Northern California. Both of these groups became the basis for Vedanta Societies in the West. Vivekananda was one of the most important philosophers and social reformers in India at the time. He was also one of the most successful and powerful Vedanta missionaries in the West.People now think of him as one of the most important people in modern India and Hinduism. Mahatma Gandhi said that after reading Vivekananda's works, he loved his country a thousand times more.

CONTENTS

The Methods And Purpose Of Religion

In studying the religions of the world we generally find two methods of procedure. The one is from God to man. That is to say, we have the Semitic group of religions in which the idea of God comes almost from the very first, and, strangely enough, without any idea of soul. It was very remarkable amongst the ancient Hebrews that, until very recent periods in their history, they never evolved any idea of a human soul. Man was composed of certain mind and material particles, and that was all. With death everything ended. But, on the other hand, there was a most wonderful idea of God evolved by the same race. This is one of the methods of procedure. The other is through man to God. The second is peculiarly Aryan, and the first is peculiarly Semitic.

The Aryan first began with the soul. His ideas of God were hazy, indistinguishable, not very clear; but, as his idea of the human soul began to be clearer, his idea of God began to be clearer in the same proportion. So the inquiry in the Vedas was always through the soul. All the knowledge the Aryans got of God was through the human soul; and, as such, the peculiar stamp that has been left upon their whole cycle of philosophy is that introspective search after divinity. The Aryan man was always seeking divinity inside his own self. It became, in course of time, natural, characteristic. It is remarkable in their art and in their commonest dealings. Even at the present time, if we take a European picture of a man in a religious attitude, the painter always makes his subject point his eyes upwards, looking outside of nature for God, looking up into the skies. In India, on the other hand, the religious attitude is always presented by making the subject close his eyes. He is, as it were, looking inward.

These are the two subjects of study for man, external and internal nature; and though at first these seem to be contradictory, yet external nature must, to the ordinary man, be entirely composed of internal nature, the world of thought. The majority of philosophies in every country, especially in the West, have started with the assumption that these two, matter and mind, are contradictory existences; but in the long run we shall find that they converge towards each other and in the end unite and form an infinite whole. So it is not that by this analysis I mean a higher or lower standpoint with regard to the subject. I do not mean that those who want to search after truth through external nature are wrong, nor that those who want to search after truth through internal nature are higher. These are the two modes of procedure. Both of them must live; both of them must be studied; and in the end we shall find that they meet. We shall see that neither is the body antagonistic to the mind, nor the mind to the body, although we find, many persons who think that this body is nothing. In old times, every country was full of people who thought this body was only a disease, a sin, or something of that kind. Later on, however, we see how, as it was taught in the Vedas, this body melts into the mind, and the mind into the body.

You must remember the one theme that runs through all the Vedas: "Just as by the knowledge of one lump of clay we know all the clay that is in the universe, so what is that, knowing which we know everything else?" This, expressed more or less clearly, is the theme of all human knowledge. It is the finding of a unity towards which we are all going. Every action of our lives — the most material, the grossest as well as the finest, the highest, the most spiritual — is alike tending towards this one ideal, the finding of unity. A man is single. He marries. Apparently it may be a selfish act, but at the same time, the impulsion, the motive power, is to find that unity. He has children, he has friends, he loves his country, he loves the world, and ends by loving the whole universe. Irresistibly we are impelled towards that perfection which consists in finding the unity, killing this little self and making ourselves broader and broader. This is the goal, the end towards which the universe is rushing. Every atom is trying to go and join itself to the next atom. Atoms after atoms combine, making huge balls, the earths, the suns, the moons, the stars, the planets. They in their turn, are trying to rush towards each other, and at last, we know that the whole universe, mental and material, will be fused into one.

The process that is going on in the cosmos on a large scale, is the same as that going on in the microcosm on a smaller scale. Just as this universe has its existence in separation, in distinction, and all the while is rushing towards unity, non-separation, so in our little worlds each soul is born, as it were, cut off from the rest of the world. The more ignorant, the more unenlightened the soul, the more it thinks that it is separate from the rest of the universe. The more ignorant the person, the more he thinks, he will die or will be born, and so forth — ideas that are an expression of this separateness. But we find that, as knowledge comes, man grows, morality is evolved and the idea of non-separateness begins. Whether men understand it or not, they are impelled by that power behind to become unselfish. That is the foundation of all morality. It is the quintessence of all ethics, preached in any language, or in any religion, or by any prophet in the world. "Be thou unselfish", "Not 'I', but 'thou'" — that is the background of all ethical codes. And what is meant by this is the recognition of non-individuality — that you are a part of me, and I of you; the recognition that in hurting you I hurt myself, and in helping you I help myself; the recognition that there cannot possibly be death for me when you live. When one worm lives in this universe, how can I die? For my life is in the life of that worm. At the same time it will teach us that we cannot leave one of our fellow-beings without helping him, that in his good consists my good.

This is the theme that runs through the whole of Vedanta, and which runs through every other religion. For, you must remember, religions divide themselves generally into three parts. There is the first part, consisting of the philosophy, the essence, the principles of every religion. These principles find expression in mythology — lives of saints or heroes, demi-gods, or gods, or divine beings; and the whole idea of this mythology is that of power. And in the lower class of mythologies — the primitive — the expression of this power is in the muscles; their heroes are strong, gigantic. One hero conquers the whole world. As man advances, he must find expression for his energy higher than in the muscles; so his heroes also find expression in something higher. The higher mythologies have heroes who are gigantic moral men. Their strength is manifested in becoming moral and pure. They can stand alone, they can beat back the surging tide of selfishness and immorality. The third portion of all religions is symbolism, which you call ceremonials and forms. Even the expression through mythology, the lives of heroes, is not sufficient for all. There are minds still lower. Like children they must have their kindergarten of religion, and these symbologies are evolved — concrete examples which they can handle and grasp and understand, which they can see and feel as material somethings.

So in every religion you find there are the three stages: philosophy, mythology, and ceremonial. There is one advantage which can be pleaded for the Vedanta, that in India, fortunately, these three stages have been sharply defined. In other religions the principles are so interwoven with the mythology that it is very hard to distinguish one from the other. The mythology stands supreme, swallowing up the principles; and in course of centuries the principles are lost sight of. The explanation, the illustration of the principle, swallows up the principle, and the people see only the explanation, the prophet, the preacher, while the principles have gone out of existence almost — so much so that even today, if a man dares to preach the principles of Christianity apart from Christ, they will try to attack him and think he is wrong and dealing blows at Christianity. In the same way, if a man wants to preach the principles of Mohammedanism, Mohammedans will think the same; because concrete ideas, the lives of great men and prophets, have entirely overshadowed the principles.

In Vedanta the chief advantage is that it was not the work of one single man; and therefore, naturally, unlike Buddhism, or Christianity, or Mohammedanism, the prophet or teacher did not entirely swallow up or overshadow the principles. The principles live, and the prophets, as it were, form a secondary group, unknown to Vedanta. The Upanishads speak of no particular prophet, but they speak of various prophets and prophetesses. The old Hebrews had something of that idea; yet we find Moses occupying most of the space of the Hebrew literature. Of course I do not mean that it is bad that these prophets should take religious hold of a nation; but it certainly is very injurious if the whole field of principles is lost sight of. We can very much agree as to principles, but not very much as to persons. The persons appeal to our emotions; and the principles, to something higher, to our calm judgement. Principles must conquer in the long run, for that is the manhood of man. Emotions many times drag us down to the level of animals. Emotions have more connection with the senses than with the faculty of reason; and, therefore, when principles are entirely lost sight of and emotions prevail, religions degenerate into fanaticism and sectarianism. They are no better than party politics and such things. The most horribly ignorant notions will be taken up, and for these ideas thousands will be ready to cut the throats of their brethren. This is the reason that, though these great personalities and prophets are tremendous motive powers for good, at the same time their lives are altogether dangerous when they lead to the disregard of the principles they represent. That has always led to fanaticism, and has deluged the world in blood. Vedanta can avoid this difficulty, because it has not one special prophet. It has many Seers, who are called Rishis or sages. Seers — that is the literal translation — those who see these truths, the Mantras.

The word Mantra means "thought out", cogitated by the mind; and the Rishi is the seer of these thoughts. They are neither the property of particular persons, nor the exclusive property of any man or woman, however great he or she may be; nor even the exclusive property of the greatest spirits — the Buddhas or Christs — whom the world has produced. They are as much the property of the lowest of the low, as they are the property of a Buddha, and as much the property of the smallest worm that crawls as of the Christ, because they are universal principles. They were never created. These principles have existed throughout time; and they will exist. They are non-create — uncreated by any laws which science teaches us today. They remain covered and become discovered, but are existing through all eternity in nature. If Newton had not been born, the law of gravitation would have remained all the same and would have worked all the same. It was Newton's genius which formulated it, discovered it, brought it into consciousness, made it a conscious thing to the human race. So are these religious laws, the grand truths of spirituality. They are working all the time. If all the Vedas and the Bibles and the Korans did not exist at all, if seers and prophets had never been born, yet these laws would exist. They are only held in abeyance, and slowly but surely would work to raise the human race, to raise human nature. But they are the prophets who see them, discover them, and such prophets are discoverers in the field of spirituality. As Newton and Galileo were prophets of physical science, so are they prophets of spirituality. They can claim no exclusive right to any one of these laws; they are the common property of all nature.

The Vedas, as the Hindus say, are eternal. We now understand what they mean by their being eternal, i.e. that the laws have neither beginning nor end, just as nature has neither beginning nor end. Earth after earth, system after system, will evolve, run for a certain time, and then dissolve back again into chaos; but the universe remains the same. Millions and millions of systems are being born, while millions are being destroyed. The universe remains the same. The beginning and the end of time can be told as regards a certain planet; but as regards the universe, time has no meaning at all. So are the laws of nature, the physical laws, the mental laws, the spiritual laws. Without beginning and without end are they; and it is within a few years, comparatively speaking, a few thousand years at best, that man has tried to reveal them. The infinite mass remains before us. Therefore the one great lesson that we learn from the Vedas, at the start, is that religion has just begun. The infinite ocean of spiritual truth lies before us to be worked on, to be discovered, to be brought into our lives. The world has seen thousands of prophets, and the world has yet to see millions.

There were times in olden days when prophets were many in every society. The time is to come when prophets will walk through every street in every city in the world. In olden times, particular, peculiar persons were, so to speak, selected by the operations of the laws of society to become prophets. The time is coming when we shall understand that to become religious means to become a prophet, that none can become religious until he or she becomes a prophet. We shall come to understand that the secret of religion is not being able to think and say all these thoughts; but, as the Vedas teach, to realise them, to realise newer and higher one than have ever been realised, to discover them, bring them to society; and the study of religion should be the training to make prophets. The schools and colleges should be training grounds for prophets. The whole universe must become prophets; and until a man becomes a prophet, religion is a mockery and a byword unto him. We must see religion, feel it, realise it in a thousand times more intense a sense than that in which we see the wall.

But there is one principle which underlies all these various manifestations of religion and which has been already mapped out for us. Every science must end where it finds a unity, because we cannot go any further. When a perfect unity is reached, that science has nothing more of principles to tell us. All the work that religions have to do is to work out the details. Take any science, chemistry, for example. Suppose we can find one element out of which we can manufacture all the other elements. Then chemistry, as a science, will have become perfect. What will remain for us is to discover every day new combinations of that one material and the application of those combinations for all the purposes of life. So with religion. The gigantic principles, the scope, the plan of religion were already discovered ages ago when man found the last words, as they are called, of the Vedas — "I am He" — that there is that One in whom this whole universe of matter and mind finds its unity, whom they call God, or Brahman, or Allah, or Jehovah, or any other name. We cannot go beyond that. The grand principle has been already mapped out for us. Our work lies in filling it in, working it out, applying it to every part of our lives. We have to work now so that every one will become a prophet. There is a great work before us.

In old times, many did not understand what a prophet meant. They thought it was something by chance, that just by a fiat of will or some superior intelligence, a man gained superior knowledge. In modern times, we are prepared to demonstrate that this knowledge is the birthright of every living being, whosoever and wheresoever he be, and that there is no chance in this universe. Every man who, we think, gets something by chance, has been working for it slowly and surely through ages. And the whole question devolves upon us: "Do we want to be prophets?" If we want, we shall be.

This, the training of prophets, is the great work that lies before us; and, consciously or unconsciously, all the great systems of religion are working toward this one great goal, only with this difference, that in many religions you will find they declare that this direct perception of spirituality is not to be had in this life, that man must die, and after his death there will come a time in another world, when he will have visions of spirituality, when he will realise things which now he must believe. But Vedanta will ask all people who make such assertions, "Then how do you know that spirituality exists?" And they will have to answer that there must have been always certain particular people who, even in this life, have got a glimpse of things which are unknown and unknowable.

Even this makes a difficulty. If they were peculiar people, haling this power simply by chance, we have no right to believe in them. It would be a sin to believe in anything that is by chance, because we cannot know it. What is meant by knowledge? Destruction of peculiarity. Suppose a boy goes into a street or a menagerie, and sees a peculiarly shaped animal. He does not know what it is. Then he goes to a country where there are hundreds like that one, and he is satisfied, he knows what the species is. Our knowledge is knowing the principle. Our non-knowledge is finding the particular without reference to principle. When we find one case or a few cases separate from the principle, without any reference to the principle, we are in darkness and do not know. Now, if these prophets, as they say, were peculiar persons who alone had the right to catch a glimpse of that which is beyond and no one else has the right, we should not believe in these prophets, because they are peculiar cases without any reference to a principle. We can only believe in them if we ourselves become prophets.

You, all of you, hear about the various jokes that get into the newspapers about the sea-serpent; and why should it be so? Because a few persons, at long intervals, came and told their stories about the sea-serpent, and others never see it. They have no particular principle to which to refer, and therefore the world does not believe. If a man comes to me and says a prophet disappeared into the air and went through it, I have the right to see that. I ask him, "Did your father or grandfather see it?" "Oh, no," he replies, "but five thousand years ago such a thing happened." And if I do not believe it, I have to be barbecued through eternity!

What a mass of superstition this is! And its effect is to degrade man from his divine nature to that of brutes. Why was reason given us if we have to believe? Is it not tremendously blasphemous to believe against reason? What right have we not to use the greatest gift that God has given to us? I am sure God will pardon a man who will use his reason and cannot believe, rather than a man who believes blindly instead of using the faculties He has given him. He simply degrades his nature and goes down to the level of the beasts — degrades his senses and dies. We must reason; and when reason proves to us the truth of these prophets and great men about whom the ancient books speak in every country, we shall believe in them. We shall believe in them when we see such prophets among ourselves. We shall then find that they were not peculiar men, but only illustrations of certain principles. They worked, and that principle expressed itself naturally, and we shall have to work to express that principle in us. They were prophets, we shall believe, when we become prophets. They were seers of things divine. They could go beyond the bounds of senses and catch a glimpse of that which is beyond. We shall believe that when we are able to do it ourselves and not before.

That is the one principle of Vedanta. Vedanta declares that religion is here and now, because the question of this life and that life, of life and death, this world and that world, is merely one of superstition and prejudice. There is no break in time beyond what we make. What difference is there between ten and twelve o'clock, except what we make by certain changes in nature? Time flows on the same. So what is meant by this life or that life? It is only a question of time, and what is lost in time may be made up by speed in work. So, says Vedanta, religion is to be realised now. And for you to become religious means that you will start without any religion work your way up and realise things, see things for yourself; and when you have done that, then, and then alone, you have religion. Before that you are no better than atheists, or worse, because the atheist is sincere — he stands up and says, "I do not know about these things — while those others do not know but go about the world, saying, "We arc very religious people." What religion they have no one knows, because they have swallowed some grandmother's story, and priests have asked them to believe these things; if they do not, then let them take care. That is how it is going.

Realisation of religion is the only way. Each one of us will have to discover. Of what use are these books, then, these Bibles of the world? They are of great use, just as maps are of a country. I have seen maps of England all my life before I came here, and they were great helps to me informing some sort of conception of England. Yet, when I arrived in this country, what a difference between the maps and the country itself! So is the difference between realisation and the scriptures. These books are only the maps, the experiences of past men, as a motive power to us to dare to make the same experiences and discover in the same way, if not better.

This is the first principle of Vedanta, that realisation is religion, and he who realises is the religious man; and he who does not is no better than he who says, "I do not know", if not worse, because the other says, "I do not know", and is sincere. In this realisation, again, we shall be helped very much by these books, not only as guides, but as giving instructions and exercises; for every science has its own particular method of investigation. You will find many persons in this world who will say. "I wanted to become religious, I wanted to realise these things, but I have not been able, so I do not believe anything." Even among the educated you will find these. Large numbers of people will tell you, "I have tried to be religious all my life, but there is nothing in it." At the same time you will find this phenomenon: Suppose a man is a chemist, a great scientific man. He comes and tells you this. If you say to him, "I do not believe anything about chemistry, because

I have all my life tried to become a chemist and do not find anything in it", he will ask, "When did you try?" "When I went to bed, I repeated, 'O chemistry, come to me', and it never came." That is the very same thing. The chemist laughs at you and says, "Oh, that is not the way. Why did you not go to the laboratory and get all the acids and alkalis and burn your hands from time to time? That alone would have taught you." Do you take the same trouble with religion? Every science has its own method of learning, and religion is to be learnt the same way. It has its own methods, and here is something we can learn, and must learn, from all the ancient prophets of the world, every one who has found something, who has realised religion. They will give us the methods, the particular methods, through which alone we shall be able to realise the truths of religion. They struggled all their lives, discovered particular methods of mental culture, bringing the mind to a certain state, the finest perception, and through that they perceived the truths of religion. To become religious, to perceive religion, feel it, to become a prophet, we have to take these methods and practice them; and then if we find nothing, we shall have the right to say, "There is nothing in religion, for I have tried and failed."

This is the practical side of all religions. You will find it in every Bible in the world. Not only do they teach principles and doctrines, but in the lives of the saints you find practices; and when it is not expressly laid down as a rule of conduct, you will always find in the lives of these prophets that even they regulated their eating and drinking sometimes. Their whole living, their practice, their method, everything was different from the masses who surrounded them; and these were the causes that gave them the higher light, the vision of the Divine. And we, if we want to have this vision, must be ready to take up these methods. It is practice, work, that will bring us up to that. The plan of Vedanta, therefore, is: first, to lay down the principles, map out for us the goal, and then to teach us the method by which to arrive at the goal, to understand and realise religion.

Again, these methods must be various. Seeing that we are so various in our natures, the same method can scarcely be applied to any two of us in the same manner. We have idiosyncrasies in our minds, each one of us; so the method ought to be varied. Some, you will find, are very emotional in their nature; some very philosophical, rational; others cling to all sorts of ritualistic forms — want things which are concrete. You will find that one man does not care for any ceremony or form or anything of the sort; they are like death to him. And another man carries a load of amulets all over his body; he is so fond of these symbols! Another man who is emotional in his nature wants to show acts of charity to everyone; he weeps, he laughs, and so on. And all of these certainly cannot have the same method. If there were only one method to arrive at truth, it would be death for everyone else who is not similarly constituted. Therefore the methods should be various. Vedanta understands that and wants to lay before the world different methods through which we can work. Take up any one you like; and if one does not suit you, another may. From this standpoint we see how glorious it is that there are so many religions in the world, how good it is that there are so many teachers and prophets, instead of there being only one, as many persons would like to have it. The Mohammedans want to have the whole world Mohammedan; the Christians, Christian; and the Buddhists, Buddhist; but Vedanta says, "Let each person in the world be separate, if you will; the one principle, the units will be behind. The more prophets there are, the more books, the more seers, the more methods, so much the better for the world." Just as in social life the greater the number of occupations in every society, the better for that society, the more chance is there for everyone of that society to make a living; so in the world of thought and of religion. How much better it is today when we have so many divisions of science — how much more is it possible for everyone to have great mental culture, with this great variety before us! How much better it is, even on the physical plane, to have the opportunity of so many various things spread before us, so that we may choose any one we like, the one which suits us best! So it is with the world of religions. It is a most glorious dispensation of the Lord that there are so many religions in the world; and would to God that these would increase every day, until every man had a religion unto himself!

Vedanta understands that and therefore preaches the one principle and admits various methods. It has nothing to say against anyone — whether you are a Christian, or a Buddhist, or a Jew, or a Hindu, whatever mythology you believe, whether you owe allegiance to the prophet of Nazareth, or of Mecca, or of India, or of anywhere else, whether you yourself are a prophet — it has nothing to say. It only preaches the principle which is the background of every religion and of which all the prophets and saints and seers are but illustrations and manifestations. Multiply your prophets if you like; it has no objection. It only preaches the principle, and the method it leaves to you. Take any path you like; follow any prophet you like; but have only that method which suits your own nature, so that you will be sure to progress.

The Nature Of The Soul And Its Goal

The earliest idea is that a man, when he dies, is not annihilated. Something lives and goes on living even after the man is dead. Perhaps it would be better to compare the three most ancient nations — the Egyptians, the Babylonians, and the ancient Hindus — and take this idea from all of them. With the Egyptians and the Babylonians, we find a sort of soul idea — that of a double. Inside this body, according to them, there is another body which is moving and working here; and when the outer body dies, the double gets out and lives on for a certain length of time; but the life of the double is limited by the preservation of the outer body. If the body which the double has left is injured in any part, the double is sure to be injured in that part. That is why we find among the ancient Egyptians such solicitude to preserve the dead body of a person by embalming, building pyramids, etc. We find both with the Babylonians and the ancient Egyptians that this double cannot live on through eternity; it can, at best, live on for a certain time only, that is, just so long as the body it has left can be preserved.

The next peculiarity is that there is an element of fear connected with this double. It is always unhappy and miserable; its state of existence is one of extreme pain. It is again and again coming back to those that are living, asking for food and drink and enjoyments that it can no more have. It is wanting to drink of the waters of the Nile, the fresh waters which it can no more drink. It wants to get back those foods it used to enjoy while in this life; and when it finds it cannot get them, the double becomes fierce, sometimes threatening the living with death and disaster if it is not supplied with such food.

Coming to Aryan thought, we at once find a very wide departure. There is still the double idea there, but it has become a sort of spiritual body; and one great difference is that the life of this spiritual body, the soul, or whatever you may call it, is not limited by the body it has left. On the contrary, it has obtained freedom from this body, and hence the peculiar Aryan custom of burning the dead. They want to get rid of the body which the person has left, while the Egyptian wants to preserve it by burying, embalming, and building pyramids. Apart from the most primitive system of doing away with the dead, amongst nations advanced to a certain extent, the method of doing away with the bodies of the dead is a great indication of their idea of the soul. Wherever we find the idea of a departed soul closely connected with the idea of the dead body, we always find the tendency to preserve the body, and we also find burying in some form or other. On the other hand, with those in whom the idea has developed that the soul is a separate entity from the body and will not be hurt if the dead body is even destroyed, burning is always the process resorted to. Thus we find among all ancient Aryan races burning of the dead, although the Parsees changed it to exposing the body on a tower. But the very name of the tower (Dakhma) means a burning-place, showing that in ancient times they also used to burn their bodies. The other peculiarity is that among the Aryans there was no element of fear with these doubles. They are not coming down to ask for food or help; and when denied that help, they do not become ferocious or try to destroy those that are living. They rather are joyful, are glad at getting free. The fire of the funeral pyre is the symbol of disintegration. The symbol is asked to take the departed soul gently up and to carry it to the place where the fathers live, where there is no sorrow, where there is joy for ever, and so on.

Of these two ideas we see at once that they are of a similar nature, the one optimistic, and the other pessimistic — being the elementary. The one is the evolution of the other. It is quite possible that the Aryans themselves had, or may have had, in very ancient times exactly the same idea as the Egyptians. In studying their most ancient records, we find the possibility of this very idea. But it is quite a bright thing, something bright. When a man dies, this soul goes to live with the fathers and lives there enjoying their happiness. These fathers receive it with great kindness; this is the most ancient idea in India of a soul. Later on, this idea becomes higher and higher. Then it was found out that what they called the soul before was not really the soul. This bright body, fine body, however fine it might be, was a body after all; and all bodies must be made up of materials, either gross or fine. Whatever had form or shape must be limited, and could not be eternal. Change is inherent in every form. How could that which is changeful be eternal? So, behind this bright body, as it were, they found something which was the soul of man. It was called the Âtman, the Self. This Self idea then began. It had also to undergo various changes. By some it was thought that this Self was eternal; that it was very minute, almost as minute as an atom; that it lived in a certain part of the body, and when a man died, his Self went away, taking along with it the bright body. There were other people who denied the atomic nature of the soul on the same ground on which they had denied that this bright body was the soul.

Out of all these various opinions rose Sânkhya philosophy, where at once we find immense differences. The idea there is that man has first this gross body; behind the gross body is the fine body, which is the vehicle of the mind, as it were; and behind even that is the Self, the Perceiver, as the Sânkhyas call it, of the mind; and this is omnipresent. That is, your soul, my soul, everyone's soul is everywhere at the same time. If it is formless, how can it be said to occupy space? Everything that occupies space has form. The formless can only be infinite. So each soul is everywhere. The second theory put forward is still more startling. They all saw in ancient times that human beings are progressive, at least many of them. They grew in purity and power and knowledge; and the question was asked: Whence was this knowledge, this purity, this strength which men manifested? Here is a baby without any knowledge. This baby grows and becomes a strong, powerful, and wise man. Whence did that baby get its wealth of knowledge and power? The answer was that it was in the soul; the soul of the baby had this knowledge and power from the very beginning. This power, this purity, this strength were in that soul, but they were unmanifested; they have become manifested. What is meant by this manifestation or unmanifestation? That each soul is pure and perfect, omnipotent and omniscient, as they say in the Sankhya; but it can manifest itself externally only according to the mind it has got. The mind is, as it were, the reflecting mirror of the soul. My mind reflects to a certain extent the powers of my soul; so your soul, and so everyone's. That mirror which is clearer reflects the soul better. So the manifestation varies according to the mind one possesses; but the souls in themselves are pure and perfect.

There was another school who thought that this could not be. Though souls are pure and perfect by their nature, this purity and perfection become, as they say, contracted at times, and expanded at other times. There are certain actions and certain thoughts which, as it were, contract the nature of the soul; and then also other thoughts and acts, which bring its nature out, manifest it. This again is explained. All thoughts and actions that make the power and purity of the soul get contracted are evil actions, evil thoughts; and all those thoughts and actions which make the soul manifest itself — make the powers come out, as it were — are good and moral actions. The difference between the two theories is very slight; it is more of less a play on the words expansion and contraction. The one that holds that the variation only depends on the mind the soul has got is the better explanation, no doubt, but the contracting and expanding theory wants to take refuge behind the two words; and they should be asked what is meant by contraction of soul, or expansion. Soul is a spirit. You can question what is meant by contraction or expansion with regard to material, whether gross which we call matter, or fine, the mind; but beyond that, if it is not matter, that which is not bound by space or by time, how to explain the words contraction and expansion with regard to that? So it seems that this theory which holds that the soul is pure and perfect all the time, only its nature is more reflected in some minds than in others, is the better. As the mind changes, its character grows, as it were, more and more clear and gives a better reflection of the soul. Thus it goes on, until the mind has become so purified that it reflects fully the quality of the soul; then the soul becomes liberated.

This is the nature of the soul. What is the goal? The goal of the soul among all the different sects in India seems to be the same. There is one idea with all, and that is liberation. Man is infinite; and this limitation in which he exists now is not his nature. But through these limitations he is struggling upward and forward until he reaches the infinite, the unlimited, his birthright, his nature. All these combinations and recombinations and manifestations that we see round us are not the aim or the goal, but merely by the way and in passing. These combinations as earths and suns, and moons and stars, right and wrong, good and bad, our laughter and our tears, our joys and sorrows, are to enable us to gain experience through which the soul manifests its perfect nature and throws off limitation. No more, then, is it bound by laws either of internal or external nature. It has gone beyond all law, beyond all limitation, beyond all nature. Nature has come under the control of the soul, not the soul under the control of nature, as it thinks it is now. That is the one goal that the soul has; and all the succeeding steps through which it is manifesting, all the successive experiences through which it is passing in order to attain to that goal — freedom — are represented as its births. The soul is, as it were, taking up a lower body and trying to express itself through that. It finds that to be insufficient, throws it aside, and a higher one is taken up. Through that it struggles to express itself. That also is found to be insufficient, is rejected, and a higher one comes; so on and on until a body is found through which the soul manifests its highest aspirations. Then the soul becomes free.

Now the question is: If the soul is infinite and exists everywhere, as it must do, if it is a spirit, what is meant by its taking up bodies and passing through body after body? The idea is that the soul neither comes nor goes, neither is born nor dies. How can the omnipresent be born? It is meaningless nonsense to say that the soul lives in a body. How can the unlimited live in a limited space? But as a man having a book in his hands reads one page and turns it over, goes to the next page, reads that, turns it over, and so on, yet it is the book that is being turned over, the pages that are revolving, and not he — he is where he is always — even so with regard to the soul. The whole of nature is that book which the soul is reading. Each life, as it were, is one page of that book; and that read, it is turned over, and so on and on, until the whole of the book is finished, and that soul becomes perfect, having got all the experiences of nature. Yet at the same time it never moved, nor came, nor went; it was only gathering experiences. But it appears to us that we are moving. The earth is moving, yet we think that the sun is moving instead of the earth, which we know to be a mistake, a delusion of the senses. So is also this, delusion that we are born and that we die, that we come or that we go. We neither come nor go, nor have we been born. For where is the soul to go? There is no place for it to go. Where is it not already?

Thus the theory comes of the evolution of nature and the manifestation of the soul. The processes of evolution, higher and higher combinations, are not in the soul; it is already what it is. They are in nature. But as nature is evolving forward into higher and higher combinations, more and more of the majesty of the soul is manifesting itself. Suppose here is a screen, and behind the screen is wonderful scenery. There is one small hole in the screen through which we can catch only a little bit of that scenery behind. Suppose that hole becomes increased in size. As the hole increases in size, more and more of the scenery behind comes within the range of vision; and when the whole screen has disappeared, there is nothing between the scenery and you; you see the whole of it. This screen is the mind of man. Behind it is the majesty, the purity, the infinite power of the soul, and as the mind becomes clearer and clearer, purer and purer, more of the majesty of the soul manifests itself. Not that the soul is changing, but the change is in the screen. The soul is the unchangeable One, the immortal, the pure, the ever-blessed One.

So, at last, the theory comes to this. From the highest to the lowest and most wicked man, in the greatest of; human beings and the lowest of crawling worms under our feet, is the soul, pure and perfect, infinite and ever-blessed. In the worm that soul is manifesting only an infinitesimal part of its power and purity, and in the greatest man it is manifesting most of it. The difference consists in the degree of manifestation, but not in the essence. Through all beings exists the same pure and perfect soul.

There are also the ideas of heavens and other places, but these are thought to be second-rate. The idea of heaven is thought to be a low idea. It arises from the desire for a place of enjoyment. We foolishly want to limit the whole universe with our present experience. Children think that the whole universe is full of children. Madmen think the whole universe a lunatic asylum, and so on. So those to whom this world is but sense-enjoyment, whose whole life is in eating and feasting, with very little difference between them and brute beasts — such are naturally found to conceive of places where they will have more enjoyments, because this life is short. Their desire for enjoyment is infinite, so they are bound to think of places where they will have unobstructed enjoyment of the senses; and we see, as we go on, that those who want to go to such places will have to go; they will dream, and when this dream is over, they will be in another dream where there is plenty of sense-enjoyment; and when that dream breaks, they will have to think of something else. Thus they will be driving about from dream to dream.

Then comes the last theory, one more idea about the soul. If the soul is pure and perfect in its essence and nature, and if every soul is infinite and omnipresent, how is it that there can be many souls? There cannot be many infinites. There cannot be two even, not to speak of many. If there were two infinites, one would limit the other, and both become finite. The infinite can only be one, and boldly the last conclusion is approached — that it is but one and not two.

Two birds are sitting on the same tree, one on the top, the other below, both of most beautiful plumage. The one eats the fruits, while the other remains, calm and majestic, concentrated in its own glory. The lower bird is eating fruits, good and evil, going after sense-enjoyments; and when it eats occasionally a bitter fruit, it gets higher and looks up and sees the other bird sitting there calm and majestic, neither caring for good fruit nor for bad, sufficient unto itself, seeking no enjoyment beyond itself. It itself is enjoyment; what to seek beyond itself? The lower bird looks at the upper bird and wants to get near. It goes a little higher; but its old impressions are upon it, and still it goes about eating the same fruit. Again an exceptionally bitter fruit comes; it gets a shock, looks up. There the same calm and majestic one! It comes near but again is dragged down by past actions, and continues to eat the sweet and bitter fruits. Again the exceptionally bitter fruit comes, the bird looks up, gets nearer; and as it begins to get nearer and nearer, the light from the plumage of the other bird is reflected upon it. Its own plumage is melting away, and when it has come sufficiently near, the whole vision changes. The lower bird never existed, it was always the upper bird, and what it took for the lower bird was only a little bit of a reflection.

Such is the nature of the soul. This human soul goes after sense-enjoyments, vanities of the world; like animals it lives only in the senses, lives only in momentary titillations of the nerves. When there comes a blow, for a moment the head reels, and everything begins to vanish, and it finds that the world was not what it thought it to be, that life was not so smooth.

It looks upward and sees the infinite Lord a moment, catches a glimpse of the majestic One, comes a little nearer, but is dragged away by its past actions. Another blow comes, and sends it back again. It catches another glimpse of the infinite Presence, comes nearer, and as it approaches nearer and nearer, it begins to find out that its individuality — its low, vulgar, intensely selfish individuality — is melting away; the desire to sacrifice the whole world to make that little thing happy is melting away; and as it gets gradually nearer and nearer, nature begins to melt away. When it has come sufficiently near, the whole vision changes, and it finds that it was the other bird, that this infinity which it had viewed as from a distance was its own Self, this wonderful glimpse that it had got of the glory and majesty was its own Self, and it indeed was that reality. The soul then finds That which is true in everything. That which is in every atom, everywhere present, the essence of all things, the God of this universe — know that thou art He, know that thou art free.

The Importance Of Psychology

The idea of psychology in the West is very much degraded. Psychology is the science of sciences; but in the West it is placed upon the same plane as all other sciences; that is, it is judged by the same criterion — utility.

How much practical benefit will it do to humanity? How much will it add to our rapidly growing happiness? How much will it detract from our rapidly increasing pain? Such is the criterion by which everything is judged in the West.

People seem to forget that about ninety per cent of all our knowledge cannot, in the very nature of things, be applied in a practical way to add to our material happiness or to lessen our misery. Only the smallest fraction of our scientific knowledge can have any such practical application to our daily lives. This is so because only an infinitely small percentage of our conscious mind is on the sensuous plane. We have just a little bit of sensuous consciousness and imagine that to be our entire mind and life; but, as a matter of fact, it is but a drop in the mighty ocean of subconscious mind. If all there is of us were a bundle of sense-perceptions, all the knowledge we could gain could be utilised in the gratification of our sense-pleasures. But fortunately such is not the case. As we get further and further away from the animal state, our sense-pleasures become less and less; and our enjoyment, in a rapidly increasing consciousness of scientific and psychological knowledge, becomes more and more intense; and "knowledge for the sake of knowledge", regardless of the amount of sense-pleasures it may conduce to, becomes the supreme pleasure of the mind.

But even taking the Western idea of utility as a criterion by which to judge, psychology, by such a standard even, is the science of sciences. Why? We are all slaves to our senses, slaves to our own minds, conscious and subconscious. The reason why a criminal is a criminal is not because he desires to be one, but because he has not his mind under control and is therefore a slave to his own conscious and subconscious mind, and to the mind of everybody else. He must follow the dominant trend of his own mind; he cannot help it; he is forced onward in spite of himself, in spite of his own better promptings, his own better nature; he is forced to obey the dominant mandate of his own mind. Poor man, he cannot help himself. We see this in our own lives constantly. We are constantly doing things against the better side of our nature, and afterwards we upbraid ourselves for so doing and wonder what we could have been thinking of, how we could do such a thing! Yet again and again we do it, and again and again we suffer for it and upbraid ourselves. At the time, perhaps, we think we desire to do it, but we only desire it because we are forced to desire it. We are forced onward, we are helpless! We are all slaves to our own and to everybody else's mind; whether we are good or bad, that makes no difference. We are led here and there because we cannot help ourselves. We say we think, we do, etc. It is not so. We think because we have to think. We act because we have to. We are slaves to ourselves and to others. Deep down in our subconscious mind are stored up all the thoughts and acts of the past, not only of this life, but of all other lives we have lived. This great boundless ocean of subjective mind is full of all the thoughts and actions of the past. Each one of these is striving to be recognised, pushing outward for expression, surging, wave after wave, out upon the objective mind, the conscious mind. These thoughts, the stored-up energy, we take for natural desires, talents, etc. It is because we do not realise their true origin. We obey them blindly, unquestioningly; and slavery, the most helpless kind of slavery, is the result; and we call ourselves free. Free! We who cannot for a moment govern our own minds, nay, cannot hold our minds on a subject, focus it on a point to the exclusion of everything else for a moment! Yet we call ourselves free. Think of it! We cannot do as we know we ought to do even for a very short space of time. Some sense-desire will crop up, and immediately we obey it. Our conscience smites us for such weakness, but again and again we do it, we are always doing it. We cannot live up to a high standard of life, try as we will. The ghosts of past thoughts, past lives hold us down. All the misery of the world is caused by this slavery to the senses. Our inability to rise above the sense-life — the striving for physical pleasures, is the cause of all the horrors and miseries in the world.

It is the science of psychology that teaches us to hold in check the wild gyrations of the mind, place it under the control of the will, and thus free ourselves from its tyrannous mandates. Psychology is therefore the science of sciences, without which all sciences and all other knowledge are worthless.

The mind uncontrolled and unguided will drag us down, down, for ever — rend us, kill us; and the mind controlled and guided will save us, free us. So it must be controlled, and psychology teaches us how to do it.

To study and analyse any material science, sufficient data are obtained. These facts are studied and analysed and a knowledge of the science is the result. But in the study and analysis of the mind, there are no data, no facts acquired from without, such as are equally at the command of all. The mind is analysed by itself. The greatest science, therefore, is the science of the mind, the science of psychology.

In the West, the powers of the mind, especially unusual powers, are looked upon as bordering on witchcraft and mysticism. The study of higher psychology has been retarded by its being identified with mere alleged psychic phenomena, as is done by some mystery-mongering order of Hindu fakirs.

Physicists obtain pretty much the same results the world over. They do not differ in their general facts, nor in the results which naturally follow from such facts. This is because the data of physical science are obtainable by all and are universally recognised, and the results are logical conclusions based upon these universally recognised facts. In the realm of the mind, it is different. Here there are no data, no facts observable by the physical senses, and no universally recognised materials therefore, from which to build a system of psychology after their being equally experimented upon by all who study the mind.

Deep, deep within, is the soul, the essential man, the Âtman. Turn the mind inward and become united to that; and from that standpoint of stability, the gyrations of the mind can be watched and facts observed, which are to be found in all persons. Such facts, such data, are to be found by those who go deep enough, and only by such. Among that large class of self-styled mystics the world over, there is a great difference of opinion as to the mind, its nature, powers, etc. This is because such people do not go deep enough. They have noticed some little activity of their own and others' minds and, without knowing anything about the real character of such superficial manifestations, have published them as facts universal in their application; and every religious and mystical crank has facts, data, etc., which, he claims, are reliable criteria for investigation, but which are in fact nothing more or less than his own imaginings

If you intend to study the mind, you must have systematic training; you must practice to bring the mind under your control, to attain to that consciousness from which you will be able to study the mind and remain unmoved by any of its wild gyrations. Otherwise the facts observed will not be reliable; they will not apply to all people and therefore will not be truly facts or data at all.

Among that class who have gone deeply into the study of the mind, the facts observed have been the same, no matter in what part of the world such persons may be or what religious belief they may have. The results obtained by all who go deep enough into the mind are the same.

The mind operates by perception and impulsion. For instance, the rays of the light enter by eyes, are carried by the nerves to the brain, and still I do not see the light. The brain then conveys the impulse to the mind, but yet I do not see the light; the mind then reacts, and the light flashes across the mind. The mind's reaction is impulsion, and as a result the eye perceives the object.

To control the mind you must go deep down into the subconscious mind, classify and arrange in order all the different impressions, thoughts, etc., stored up there, and control them. This is the first step. By the control of the subconscious mind you get control over the conscious.

Nature And Man

The modern idea of nature includes only that part of the universe that is manifested on the physical plane. That which is generally understood to be mind is not considered to be nature.

Philosophers endeavouring to prove the freedom of the will have excluded the mind from nature; for as nature is bound and governed by law, strict unbending law, mind, if considered to be in nature, would be bound by law also. Such a claim would destroy the doctrine of free will; for how can that be free which is bound by law?

The philosophers of India have taken the reverse stand. They hold all physical life, manifest and unmanifest, to be bound by law. The mind as well as external nature, they claim, is bound by law, and by one and the same law. If mind is not bound by law, if the thoughts we think are not the necessary results of preceding thoughts, if one mental state is not followed by another which it produces, then mind is irrational; and who can claim free will and at the same time deny the operation of reason? And on the other hand, who can admit that the mind is governed by the law of causation and claim that the will is free?

Law itself is the operation of cause and effect. Certain things happen according to certain other things which have gone before. Every precedent has its consequent. Thus it is in nature. If this operation of law obtains in the mind, the mind is bound and is therefore not free. No, the will is not free. How can it be? But we all know, we all feel, that one are free. Life would have no meaning, it would not be worth living, if we were not free.

The Eastern philosophers accepted this doctrine, or rather propounded it, that the mind and the will are within time, space, and causation, the same as so-called matter; and that they are therefore bound by the law of causation. We think in time; our thoughts are bound by time; all that exists, exists in time and space. All is bound by the law of causation.

Now that which we call matter and mind are one and the same substance. The only difference is in the degree of vibration. Mind at a very low rate of vibration is what is known as matter. Matter at a high rate of vibration is what is known as mind. Both are the same substance; and therefore, as matter is bound by time and space and causation, mind which is matter at a high rate of vibration is bound by the same law.

Nature is homogeneous. Differentiation is in manifestation. The Sanskrit word for nature is Prakriti, and means literally differentiation. All is one substance, but it is manifested variously.

Mind becomes matter, and matter in its turn becomes mind, it is simply a question of vibration.

Take a bar of steel and charge it with a force sufficient to cause it to vibrate, and what would happen? If this were done in a dark room, the first thing you would be aware of would be a sound, a humming sound. Increase the force, and the bar of steel would become luminous; increase it still more, and the steel would disappear altogether. It would become mind.

Take another illustration: If I do not eat for ten days, I cannot think. Only a few stray thoughts are in my mind. I am very weak and perhaps do not know my own name. Then I eat some bread, and in a little while I begin to think; my power of mind has returned. The bread has become mind. Similarly, the mind lessens its rate of vibration and manifests itself in the body, becomes matter.

As to which is first — matter or mind, let me illustrate: A hen lays an egg; the egg brings out another hen; that hen lays another egg; that egg brings out another hen, and so on in an endless chain. Now which is first — the egg or the hen? You cannot think of an egg that was not laid by a hen, or a hen that was not hatched out of an egg. It makes no difference which is first. Nearly all our ideas run themselves into the hen and egg business.

The greatest truths have been forgotten because of their very simplicity. Great truths are simple because they are of universal application. Truth itself is always simple. Complexity is due to man's ignorance.

Man's free agency is not of the mind, for that is bound. There is no freedom there. Man is not mind, he is soul. The soul is ever free, boundless, and eternal. Herein is man's freedom, in the soul. The soul is always free, but the mind identifying itself with its own ephemeral waves, loses sight of the soul and becomes lost in the maze of time, space, and causation — Maya.

This is the cause of our bondage. We are always identifying ourselves with the mind, and the mind's phenomenal changes.

Man's free agency is established in the soul, and the soul, realising itself to be free, is always asserting the fact in spite of the mind's bondage: "I am free! I am what I am! I am what I am!" This is our freedom. The soul — ever free, boundless, eternal — through aeons and aeons is manifesting itself more and more through its instrument, the mind.

What relation then does man bear to nature? From the lowest form of life to man, the soul is manifesting itself through nature. The highest manifestation of the soul is involved in the lowest form of manifest life and is working itself outward through the process called evolution.

The whole process of evolution is the soul's struggle to manifest itself. It is a constant struggle against nature. It is a struggle against nature, and not conformity to nature that makes man what he is. We hear a great deal about living in harmony with nature, of being in tune with nature. This is a mistake. This table, this pitcher, the minerals, a tree, are all in harmony with nature. Perfect harmony there, no discord. To be in harmony with nature means stagnation, death. How did man build this house? By being in harmony with nature? No. By fighting against nature. It is the constant struggle against nature that constitutes human progress, not conformity with it.

Concentration And Breathing

The main difference between men and the animals is the difference in their power of concentration. All success in any line of work is the result of this. Everybody knows something about concentration. We see its results every day. High achievements in art, music, etc., are the results of concentration. An animal has very little power of concentration. Those who have trained animals find much difficulty in the fact that the animal is constantly forgetting what is told him. He cannot concentrate his mind long upon anything at a time. Herein is the difference between man and the animals — man has the greater power of concentration. The difference in heir power of concentration also constitutes the difference between man and man. Compare the lowest with the highest man. The difference is in the degree of concentration. This is the only difference.

Everybody's mind becomes concentrated at times. We all concentrate upon those things we love, and we love those things upon which we concentrate our minds. What mother is there that does not love the face of her homeliest child? That face is to her the most beautiful in the world. She loves it because she concentrates her mind on it; and if every one could concentrate his mind on that same face, every one would love it. It would be to all the most beautiful face. We all concentrate our minds upon those things we love. When we hear beautiful music, our minds become fastened upon it, and we cannot take them away. Those who concentrate their minds upon what you call classical music do not like common music, and vice versa. Music in which the notes follow each other in rapid succession holds the mind readily. A child loves lively music, because the rapidity of the notes gives the mind no chance to wander. A man who likes common music dislikes classical music, because it is more complicated and requires a greater degree of concentration to follow it.

The great trouble with such concentrations is that we do not control the mind; it controls us. Something outside of ourselves, as it were, draws the mind into it and holds it as long as it chooses. We hear melodious tones or see a beautiful painting, and the mind is held fast! We cannot take it away.

If I speak to you well upon a subject you like, your mind becomes concentrated upon what I am saying. I draw your mind away from yourself and hold it upon the subject in spite of yourself. Thus our attention is held, our minds are concentrated upon various things, in spite of ourselves. We cannot help it.

Now the question is: Can this concentration be developed, and can we become masters of it? The Yogis say, yes. The Yogis say that we can get perfect control of the mind. On the ethical side there is danger in the development of the power of concentration — the danger of concentrating the mind upon an object and then being unable to detach it at will. This state causes great suffering. Almost all our suffering is caused by our not having the power of detachment. So along with the development of concentration we must develop the power of detachment. We must learn not only to attach the mind to one thing exclusively, but also to detach it at a moment's notice and place it upon something else. These two should be developed together to make it safe.

This is the systematic development of the mind. To me the very essence of education is concentration of mind, not the collecting of facts. If I had to do my education over again, and had any voice in the matter, I would not study facts at all. I would develop the power of concentration and detachment, and then with a perfect instrument I could collect facts at will. Side by side, in the child, should be developed the power of concentration and detachment.

My development has been one-sided all along I developed concentration without the power of detaching my mind at will; and the most intense suffering of my life has been due to this. Now I have the power of detachment, but I had to learn it in later life.

We should put our minds on things; they should not draw our minds to them. We are usually forced to concentrate. Our minds are forced to become fixed upon different things by an attraction in them which we cannot resist. To control the mind, to place it just where we want it, requires special training. It cannot be done in any other way. In the study of religion the control of the mind is absolutely necessary. We have to turn the mind back upon itself in this study.

In training the mind the first step is to begin with the breathing. Regular breathing puts the body in a harmonious condition; and it is then easier to reach the mind. In practicing breathing, the first thing to consider is Âsana or posture. Any posture in which a person can sit easily is his proper position. The spine should be kept free, and the weight of the body should be supported by the ribs. Do not try by contrivances to control the mind; simple breathing is all that is necessary in that line. All austerities to gain concentration of the mind are a mistake. Do not practice them.

The mind acts on the body, and the body in its turn acts upon the mind. They act and react upon each other. Every mental state creates a corresponding state in the body, and every action in the body has its corresponding effect on the mind. It makes no difference whether you think the body and mind are two different entities, or whether you think they are both but one body — the physical body being the gross part and the mind the fine part. They act and react upon each other. The mind is constantly becoming the body. In the training of the mind, it is easier to reach it through the body. The body is easier to grapple with than the mind.

The finer the instrument, the greater the power. The mind is much finer and more powerful than the body. For this reason it is easier to begin with the body.

The science of breathing is the working through the body to reach the mind. In this way we get control of the body, and then we begin to feel the finer working of the body, the finer and more interior, and so on till we reach the mind. As we feel the finer workings of the body, they come under our control. After a while you will be able to feel the operation of the mind on the body. You will also feel the working of one half of the mind upon the other half, and also feel the mind recruiting the nerve centres; for the mind controls and governs the nervous system. You will feel the mind operating along the different nerve currents.

Thus the mind is brought under control — by regular systematic breathing, by governing the gross body first and then the fine body.

The first breathing exercise is perfectly safe and very healthful. It will give you good health, and better your condition generally at least. The other practices should be taken up slowly and carefully.

Introduction To Jnana-Yoga

This is the rational and philosophic side of Yoga and very difficult, but I will take you slowly through it.

Yoga means the method of joining man and God. When you understand this, you can go on with your own definitions of man and God, and you will find the term Yoga fits in with every definition. Remember always, there are different Yogas for different minds, and that if one does not suit you, another may. All religions are divided into theory and practice. The Western mind has given itself up to the theory and only sees the practical part of religion as good works. Yoga is the practical part of religion and shows that religion is a practical power apart from good works.

At the beginning of the nineteenth century man tried to find God through reason, and Deism was the result. What little was left of God by this process was destroyed by Darwinism and Millism. Men were then thrown back upon historical and comparative religion. They thought, religion was derived from element worship (see Max Müller on the sun myths etc.); others thought that religion was derived from ancestor worship (see Herbert Spencer). But taken as a whole, these methods have proved a failure. Man cannot get at Truth by external methods.

"If I know one lump of clay, I know the whole mass of clay." The universe is all built on the same plan. The individual is only a part, like the lump of clay. If we know the human soul — which is one atom — its beginning and general history, we know the whole of nature. Birth, growth, development, decay, death — this is the sequence in all nature and is the same in the plant and the man. The difference is only in time. The whole cycle may be completed in one case in a day, in the other in three score years and ten; the methods are the same. The only way to reach a sure analysis of the universe is by the analysis of our own minds. A proper psychology is essential to the understanding of religion. To reach Truth by reason alone is impossible, because imperfect reason cannot study its own fundamental basis. Therefore the only way to study the mind is to get at facts, and then intellect will arrange them and deduce the principles. The intellect has to build the house; but it cannot do so without bricks and *it* cannot make bricks. Jnana-Yoga is the surest way of arriving at facts.

First we have the physiology of mind. We have organs of the senses, which are divided into organs of action and organs of perception. By organs I do not mean the external sense-instruments. The ophthalmic centre in the brain is the organ of sight, not the eye alone. So with every organ, the function is internal. Only when the mind reacts, is the object truly perceived. The sensory and motor nerves are necessary to perception.

Then there is the mind itself. It is like a smooth lake which when struck, say by a stone, vibrates. The vibrations gather together and react on the stone, and all through the lake they will spread and be felt. The mind is like the lake; it is constantly being set in vibrations, which leave an impression on the mind; and the idea of the Ego, or personal self, the "I", is the result of these impressions. This "I" therefore is only the very rapid transmission of force and is in itself no reality.

The mind-stuff is a very fine material instrument used for taking up the Prâna. When a man dies, the body dies; but a little bit of the mind, the seed, is left when all else is shattered; and this is the seed of the new body called by St. Paul "the spiritual body". This theory of the materiality of the mind accords with all modern theories. The idiot is lacking in intelligence because his mind-stuff is injured. Intelligence cannot be in matter nor can it be produced by any combinations of matter. Where then is intelligence? It is behind matter; it is the Jiva, the real Self, working through the instrument of matter. Transmission of force is not possible without matter, and as the Jiva cannot travel alone, some part of mind is left as a transmitting medium when all else is shattered by death.

How are perceptions made? The wall opposite sends an impression to me, but I do not see the wall until my mind reacts, that is to say, the mind cannot know the wall by mere sight. The reaction that enables the mind to get a perception of the wall is an intellectual process. In this way the whole universe is seen through our eyes plus mind (or perceptive faculty); it is necessarily coloured by our own individual tendencies. The *real* wall, or the *real* universe, is outside the mind, and is unknown and unknowable. Call this universe X, and our statement is that the seen universe is X plus mind.

What is true of the external must also apply to the internal world. Mind also wants to know itself, but this Self can only be known through the medium of the mind and is, like the wall, unknown. This self we may call Y. and the statement would then be, Y plus mind is the inner self. Kant was the first to arrive at this analysis of mind, but it was long ago stated in the Vedas. We have thus, as it were, mind standing between X and Y and reacting on both.

If X is unknown, then any qualities we give to it are only derived from our own mind. Time, space, and causation are the three conditions through which mind perceives. Time is the condition for the transmission of thought, and space for the vibration of grosser matter. Causation is the sequence in which vibrations come. Mind can only cognise through these. Anything therefore, beyond mind must be beyond time, space, and causation.

To the blind man the world is perceived by touch and sound. To us with five senses it is another world. If any of us developed an electric sense and the faculty seeing electric waves, the world would appear different. Yet the world, as the X to all of these, is still the same. As each one brings his own mind, he sees his own world. There is X plus one sense; X plus two senses, up to five, as we know humanity. The result is constantly varied, yet X remains always unchanged. Y is also beyond our minds and beyond time, space, and causation.

But, you may ask, "How do we know there are two things (X and Y) beyond time, space, and causation?" Quite true, time makes differentiation, so that, as both are really beyond time, they must be really one. When mind sees this *one*, it calls it variously — X, when it is the outside world, and Y, when it is the inside world. This unit exists and is looked at through the lens of minds.

The Being of perfect nature, universally appearing to us, is God, is Absolute. The undifferentiated is the perfect condition; all others must be lower and not permanent.

What makes the undifferentiated appear differentiated to mind? This is the same kind of question as what is the origin of evil and free will? The question itself is contradictory and impossible, because the question takes for granted cause and effect. There is no cause and effect in the undifferentiated; the question assumes that the undifferentiated is in the same condition as the differentiated. "Whys" and "wherefores" are in mind only. The Self is beyond causation, and It alone is free. Its light it is which percolates through every form of mind. With every action I assert I am free, and yet every action proves that I am bound. The real Self is free, yet when mixed with mind and body, It is not free. The will is the first manifestation of the real Self; the first limitation therefore of this real Self is the will. Will is a compound of Self and mind. Now, no compound can be permanent, so that when we will to live, we must die. Immortal life is a contradiction in terms, for life, being a compound, cannot be immortal. True Being is undifferentiated and *eternal*. How does this Perfect Being become mixed up with will, mind, thought — all defective things? It never has become mixed. You are the real you (the Y of our former statement); you never were will; you never have changed; you as a person never existed; It is illusion. Then on what, you will say, do the phenomena of illusion rest? This is a bad question. Illusion never rests on Truth, but only on illusion. Everything struggles to go back to what was before these illusions, to be free in fact. What then is the value of life? It is to give us experience. Does this view do away with evolution? On the contrary, it explains it. It is really the process of refinement of matter allowing the real Self to manifest Itself. It is as if a screen or a veil were between us and some other object. The object becomes clear as the screen is gradually withdrawn. The question is simply one of manifestation of the higher Self.

The Vedanta Philosophy And Christianity

*(Notes of a lecture delivered at the Unitarian Church,
in Oakland, California, on February 28, 1900)*

Between all great religions of the world there are many points of similarity; and so startling is this likeness, at times, as to suggest the idea that in many particulars the different religions have copied from one another.

This act of imitation has been laid at the door of different religions; but that it is a superficial charge is evident from the following facts:

Religion is fundamental in the very soul of humanity; and as all life is the evolution of that which is within, it, of necessity, expresses itself through various peoples and nations.

The language of the soul is one, the languages of nations are many; their customs and methods of life are widely different. Religion is of the soul and finds expression through various nations, languages, and customs. Hence it follows that the difference between the religions of the world is one of expression and not of substance; and their points of similarity and unity are of the soul, are intrinsic, as the language of the soul is one, in whatever peoples and under whatever circumstances it manifests itself. The same sweet harmony is vibrant there also, as it is on many and diverse instruments.

The first thing in common in all great religions of the world is the possession of an authentic book. When religious systems have failed to have such a book, they have become extinct. Such was the fact of the religions of Egypt. The authentic book is the hearthstone, so to speak, of each great religious system, around which its adherents gather, and from which radiates the energy and life of the system.

Each religion, again, lays the claim that its particular book is the only authentic word of God; that all other sacred books are false and are impositions upon poor human credulity; and that to follow another religion is to be ignorant and spiritually blind.

Such bigotry is characteristic of the orthodox element of all religions. For instance, the orthodox followers of the Vedas claim that the Vedas are the only authentic word of God in the world; that God has spoken to the world only through the Vedas; not only that, but that the world itself exists by virtue of the Vedas. Before the world was, the Vedas were. Everything in the world exists because it is in the Vedas. A cow exists because the name cow is in the Vedas; that is, because the animal we know as a cow is mentioned in the Vedas. The language of the Vedas is the original language of God, all other languages are mere dialects and not of God. Every word and syllable in the Vedas must be pronounced correctly, each sound must be given its true vibration, and every departure from this rigid exactness is a terrible sin and unpardonable.

Thus, this kind of bigotry is predominant in the orthodox element of all religions. But this fighting over the letter is indulged in only by the ignorant, the spiritually blind. All who have actually attained any real religious nature never wrangle over the form in which the different religions are expressed. They know that the life of all religions is the same, and, consequently, they have no quarrel with anybody because he does not speak the same tongue.

The Vedas are, in fact, the oldest sacred books in the world. Nobody knows anything about the time when they were written or by whom. They are contained in many volumes, and I doubt that any one man ever read them all.

The religion of the Vedas is the religion of the Hindus, and the foundation of all Oriental religions; that is, all other Oriental religions are offshoots of the Vedas; all Eastern systems of religion have the Vedas as authority.

It is an irrational claim to believe in the teachings of Jesus Christ and at the same time to hold that the greater part of his teachings have no application at the present time. If you say that the reason why the powers do not follow them that believe (as Christ said they would) is because you have not faith enough and are not pure enough — that will be all right. But to say that they have no application at the present time is to be ridiculous.

I have never seen the man who was not at least my equal. I have travelled all over the world; I have been among the very worst kind of people — among cannibals — and I have never seen the man who is not at least my equal. I have done as they do — when I was a fool. Then I did not know any better; now I do. Now they do not know any better; after a while they will. Every one acts according to his own nature. We are all in process of growth. From this standpoint one man is not better than another.

Worshipper And Worshipped

(This lecture is reproduced from the
Vedanta and the West. See Vol. IV.)

(Delivered in San Francisco area, April 9, 1900)

We have been taking up the more analytical side of human nature. In this course we [shall] study the emotional side. . . . The former deals with man as unlimited being, [as] principle, the latter with man as limited being. . . . The one has no time to stop for a few tear-drops or pangs; the other cannot proceed without wiping the tear-drop, without healing that misery. One is great, so great and grand that sometimes we are staggered by the magnitude; the other [is] commonplace, and yet most beautiful and dear to us. One gets hold of us, takes us up to the heights where our lungs almost burst. We cannot breathe [in] that atmosphere. The other leaves us where we are and tries to see the objects of life, [takes the limited] view. One will accept nothing until it has the shining seal of reason; the other has faith, and what it cannot see it believes. Both are necessary. A bird cannot fly with only one wing. . . .

What we want is to see the man who is harmoniously developed . . . great in heart, great in mind, [great in deed] . . . . We want the man whose heart feels intensely the miseries and sorrows of the world. . . . And [we want] the man who not only can feel but can find the meaning of things, who delves deeply into the heart of nature and understanding. [We want] the man who will not even stop there, [but] who wants to work out [the feeling and meaning by actual deeds]. Such a combination of head, heart, and hand is what we want. There are many teachers in this world, but you will find [that most of them] are one-sided. [One] sees the glorious midday sun of intellect [and] sees nothing else. Another hears the beautiful music of love and can hear nothing else. Another is [immersed] in activity, and has neither time to feel nor time to think. Why not [have] the giant who is equally active, equally knowing, and equally loving? Is it impossible? Certainly not. This is the man of the future, of whom there are [only a] few at present. [The number of such will increase] until the whole world is humanised.

I have been talking to you so long about intellect [and] reason. We have heard the whole of Vedanta. The veil of Maya breaks: wintry clouds vanish, and the sunlight shines on us. I have been trying to climb the heights of the Himalayas, where the peaks disappear beyond the clouds. I propose lip study with you the other side: the most beautiful valleys, the most marvellous exquisiteness in nature. [We shall study the] love that holds us here in spite of all the miseries of the world, [the] love that has made us forge the chain of misery, this eternal martyrdom which man is suffering willingly, of his own accord. We want to study that for which man has forged the chain with his own hands, that for which he suffers, that eternal love. We do not mean to forget the other. The glacier of the Himalayas must join hands with the rice fields of Kashmir. The thunderbolt must blend its base note with the warbling of the birds.

This course will have to do with everything exquisite and beautiful. Worship is everywhere, in every soul. Everyone worships God. Whatever be the name, they are all worshipping God. The beginnings of worship — like the beautiful lotus, like life itself — are in the dirt of the earth. . . . There is the element of fear. There is the hungering for this world's gain. There is the worship of the beggar. These are the beginnings of [the] world worshipping, [culminating in] loving God and worshipping God through man.

Is there any God? Is there anyone to be loved, any such one capable of being loved? Loving the stone would not be much good. We only love that which understands love, that which draws our love. So with worship. Never say [that] there is a man in this world of ours who worshipped a piece of stone [as stone]. He always worshipped [the omnipresent being in the stone].

We find out that the omnipresent being is in us. [But] how can we worship, unless that being is separate from us? I can only worship Thee, and not me. I can only pray to Thee, and not me. Is there any "Thou"?

The One becomes many. When we see the One, any limitations reflected through Maya disappear; but it is quite true that the manifold is not valueless. It is through the many that we reach the one. . . .

Is there any Personal God — a God who thinks, who understands, a God who guides us? There is. The Impersonal God cannot have any one of these attributes. Each one of you is an individual: you think, you love, [you] hate, [you] are angry, sorry, etc.; yet you are impersonal, unlimited. [You are] personal and impersonal in one. You have the personal and the impersonal aspects. That [impersonal reality] cannot be angry, [nor] sorry, [nor] miserable — cannot even think misery. It cannot think, cannot know. It is knowledge itself. But the personal [aspect] knows, thinks, and dies, etc. Naturally the universal Absolute must have two aspects; the one representing the infinite reality of all things; the other, a personal aspect, the Soul of our souls, Lord of all lords. [It is] He who creates this universe. Under [His] guidance this universe exists. . . .

He, the Infinite, the Ever-Pure, the Ever-[Free,]. . . He is no judge, God cannot be [a] judge. He does not sit upon a throne and judge between the good and the wicked. . . . He is no magistrate, [no] general, [nor] master. Infinitely merciful, infinitely loving is the Personal [God].

Take it from another side. Every cell in your body has a soul conscious of the cell. It is a separate entity. It has a little will of its own, a little sphere of action of its own. All [cells] combined make up an individual. [In the same way,] the Personal God of the universe is made up of all these [many individuals].

Take it from another side. You, as I see you, are as much of your absolute nature as has been limited and perceived by one. I have limited you in order to see you through the power of my eyes, my senses. As much of you as my eyes can see, I see. As much of you as my mind can grasp is what I know to be you, and nothing more. In the same way, I am reading the Absolute, the Impersonal [and see Him as Personal]. As long as we have body and mind, we always see this triune being: God, nature, and soul. There must always be the three in one, inseparable. . . . There is nature. There are human souls. There is again That in which nature and the human souls [are contained]

The universal soul has become embodied. My soul itself is a part of God. He is the eye of our eves, the life of our life, the mind of our mind, the soul of our soul. This is the highest ideal of the Personal God we can have.

If you are not a dualist, [but are] a monist, you can still have the Personal God. . . . There is the One without a second. That One wanted to love Himself. Therefore, out of that One, He made [many]. . . . It is the big Me, the real Me, that that little me is worshipping. Thus in all systems you can have the Personal [God].

Some people are born under circumstances that make them happier than others: why should this be in the reign of a just being? There is mortality in this world. These are the difficulties in the way [These problems] have never been answered. They cannot be answered from any dualistic plane. We have to go back to philosophy to treat things as they are. We are suffering from our own Karma. It is not the fault of God. What we do is our own fault, nothing else. Why should God be blamed?. . .

Why is there evil? The only way you can solve [the problem] is [by saying that God is] the cause of both good and evil. The great difficulty in the theory of the Personal God is that if you say He is only good and not evil, you will be caught in the trap of your own argument. How do you know there is [a] God? You say [that He is] the Father of this universe, and you say He is good; and because there is [also] evil in the world, God must be evil. . . . The same difficulty!

There is no good, and there is no evil. God is all there is . . . . How do you know what is good? You feel [it]. [How do you know what is evil ? If evil comes, you feel it. . . . We know good and evil by our feelings. There is not one man who feels only good, happy feelings. There is not one who feels only unhappy feelings. . . .

Want and anxiety are the causes of all unhappiness and happiness too. Is want increasing or decreasing? Is life becoming simple or complex? Certainly complex. Wants are being multiplied. Your great-grandfathers did not want the same dress or the same amount of money [you do]. They had no electric cars, [nor] railroads, etc. That is why they had to work less. As soon as these things come, the want arises, and you have to work harder. More and more anxiety, and more and more competition.

It is very hard work to get money. It is harder work to keep it. You fight the whole world to get a little money together [and] fight all your life to protect it. [Therefore] there is more anxiety for the rich than for the poor. . . . This is the way it is. . . .

There are good and evil every where in this world. Sometimes evil becomes good, true; but other times good becomes evil also. All our senses produce evil some time or other. Let a man drink wine. It is not bad [at first], but let him go on drinking, [and] it will produce evil. . . . A man is born of rich parents; good enough. He becomes a fool, never exercises his body or brain. That is good producing evil. Think of this love of life: We go away and jump about and live a few moments; we work hard. We are born babies, entirely incapable. It takes us years to understand things again. At sixty or seventy we open our eyes, and then comes the word, "Get out! " And there you are.

We have seen that good and evil are relative terms. The thing [that is] good for me is bad for you. If you eat the dinner that I eat, you will begin to weep, and I shall laugh. . . . We [may] both dance, but I with joy and you with pain. . . . The same thing is good at one part of our life and bad at another part. How can you say [that] good and evil are all cut and dried — [that] this is all good and that is all evil?

Now, who is responsible for all this good and evil, if God is ever the good? The Christians and the Mohammedans say there is a gentleman called Satan. How can you say there are two gentlemen working? There must be one. . . . The fire that burns the child also cooks the meal. How can you call the fire good or bad, and how can you say it was created by two different persons? Who creates all [so-called] evil? God. There is no other way out. He sends death and life, plague and epidemics, and everything. If such is God, He is the good; He is the evil; He is the beautiful; He is the terrible; He is life; and He is death.

How can such a God be worshipped? We shall come to [understand] how the soul can really learn to worship the terrible; then that soul will have peace. . . . Have you peace? Do you get rid of anxieties? Turn around, first of all, and face the terrible. Tear aside the mask and find the same [God]. He is the personal — all that is [apparently] good and all that is [apparently] bad. There is none else. If there were two Gods, nature could not stand a moment. There is not another one in nature. It is all harmony. If God played one side and the devil the other, the whole [of] nature would be [in chaos]. Who can break the law? If I break this glass, it will fall down. If anyone succeeds in throwing one atom out of place, every other atom will go out of balance. . . . The law can never be broken. Each atom is kept in its place. Each is weighed and measured and fulfils its [purpose] and place. Through His command the winds blow, the sun shines. Through His rule the worlds are kept in place. Through His orders death is sporting upon the earth. Just think of two or three Gods having a wrestling match in this world! It cannot be.

We now come to see that we can have the Personal God, the creator of this universe, who is merciful and also cruel. . . . He is the good, He is the evil. He smiles, and He frowns. And none can go beyond His law. He is the creator of this universe.

What is meant by creation, something coming out of nothing? Six thousand years ago God woke up from His dream and created the world [and] before that there was nothing? What was God doing then, taking a good nap? God is the cause of the universe, and we can know the cause through the effect. If the effect is not present, the cause is not [the] cause. The cause is always known in and through the effect. . . . Creation is infinite. . . . You cannot think of the beginning in time or in space.

Why does He create it? Because He likes to; because He is free. . . . You and I are bound by law, because we can work [only] in certain ways and not in others. "Without hands, He can grasp everything. Without feet, [He moves fast]." Without body, He is omnipotent. "Whom no eyes can see, but who is the cause of sight in every eye, know Him to be the Lord." You cannot worship anything else. God is the omnipotent supporter of this universe. What is called "law" is the manifestation of His will. He rules the universe by His laws.

So far [we have discussed] God and nature, eternal God and eternal nature. What about souls? They also are eternal. No soul was [ever] created; neither can [the] soul die. Nobody can even imagine his own death. The soul is infinite, eternal. How can it die? It changes bodies. As a man takes off his old, worn-out garments and puts on new and fresh ones, even so the worn-out body is thrown away and [a] fresh body is taken.

What is the nature of the soul? The soul is also [omnipotent] and omnipresent. Spirit has neither length, nor breadth, nor thickness. . . . How can it be said to be here and there? This body falls; [the soul] works [through] another body. The soul is a circle of which the circumference is nowhere, but the centre is in the body. God is a circle whose circumference is nowhere, but whose centre is everywhere. The soul by its [very] nature is blessed, pure, and perfect; it could never be pure if its nature was impure. . . . The soul's nature is purity; that is why souls [can] become pure. It is blessed [by nature]; that is why it [can] become blessed. It is peace; [that is why it can become peaceful]. . . .

All of us who find ourselves in this plane, attracted to the body, work hard for a living, with jealousies and quarrels and hardships, and then death. That shows we are not what we should be. We are not free, perfectly pure, and so on. The soul, as it were, has become degraded. Then what the soul requires is expansion. . . .

How can you do it? Can you work it out yourself ? No. If a man's face is dusty, can you wash it out with dust? If I put a seed in the ground, the seed produces a tree, the tree produces a seed, the seed another tree, etc. Hen and egg, egg and hen. If you do something good, you will have to reap the result of that, be born again and be sorry. Once started in this infinite chain, you cannot stop. You go on, . . . up and down, [to] heavens and earths, and all these [bodies]. . . . There is no way out.

Then how can you get out of all this, and what are you here for? One idea is to get rid of misery. We are all struggling day and night to get rid of misery. . . . We cannot do it by work. Work will produce more work. It is only possible if there is someone who is free himself and lends us a hand. "Hear, ye children of immortality, all those that reside in this plane and all those that reside in the heavens above, I have found the secret", says the great sage. "I have found Him who is beyond all darkness. Through His mercy alone we cross this ocean of life."

In India, the idea of the goal is this: There are heavens, there are hells, there are earths, but they are not permanent. If I am sent to hell, it is not permanent. The same struggle goes on and on wherever I am. How to get beyond all this struggle is the problem. If I go to heaven, perhaps there will be a little bit of rest. If I get punished for my misdeeds, that cannot last [for ever either] . . . . The Indian ideal is not to go to heaven. Get out of this earth, get out of hell, and get out of heaven! What is the goal? It is freedom. You must all be free. The glory of the soul is covered up. It has to be uncovered again. The soul exists. It is everywhere. Where shall it go? . . . Where can it go? It can only go where it is not. If you understand [that] it is ever present, . . . [there will be] perfect happiness for ever afterwards. No more births and deaths. . . . No more disease, no body. [The] body itself is the biggest disease. . . .

The soul shall stand [as] soul. Spirit shall live as spirit. How is this to be done? By worshipping [the Lord in] the soul, who, by his [very] nature is ever present, pure, and perfect. There cannot be two almighty beings in this world. [Imagine having] two or three Gods; one will create the world, another says, "I will destroy the world." It [can] never happen. There must be one God. The soul attains to perfection; [it becomes] almost omnipotent [and] omniscient. This is the worshipper. Who is the worshipped? He, the Lord God Himself, the Omnipresent, the Omniscient, and so on. And above all, He is Love. How is [the soul] to attain this perfection? By worship.

(Vedanta and the West, July-Aug. 1955).

Formal Worship

(This lecture is reproduced from the
Vedanta and the West. See Vol. IV.)

(Delivered in San Francisco area, April 10, 1900)

All of you who are students of the Bible . . . .understand that the whole
[of] Jewish history and Jewish' thought have been produced by two [types
of] teachers — priests and prophets, the priests representing the power
of conservatism, the prophets the power of progress. The whole thing is
that a conservative ritualism creeps in; formality gets hold of everything.
This is true of every country and every religion. Then come some new
seers with new visions; they preach new ideals and ideas and give a new
push to society. In a few generations the followers become so faithful to
their masters' ideas that they cannot see anything else. The most advanced,
liberal preachers of this age within a few years will be the most conservative
priests. The advanced thinkers, in their turn, will begin to hinder the man
who goes a little farther. They will not let anyone go farther than what they
themselves have attained. They are content to leave things as they are.

The power which works through the formative principles of every
religion in every country is manifested in the forms of religion. . . . Principles
and books, certain rules and movements — standing up, sitting down — all
these belong to the same category of worship Spiritual worship becomes
materialised in order that the majority of mankind can get hold of it. The
vast majority of mankind in every country are never [seen] to worship spirit
as spirit. It is not yet possible. I do not know if there ever will be a time
when they can. How many thousands in this city are ready to worship God
as spirit? Very few. They cannot; they live in the senses. You have to give
them cut and dried ideas. Tell them to do something physical: Stand up
twenty times; sit down twenty times. They will understand that. Tell them
to breathe in through one nostril and breathe out through the other. They
will understand that. All this idealism about spirit they cannot accept at all.
It is not their fault. . . . If you have the power to worship God as spirit, good!
But there was a time when you could not. . . . If the people are crude, the
religious conceptions are crude, and the forms are uncouth and gross. If the

people are refined and cultured, the forms are more beautiful. There must be forms, only the forms change according to the times.

It is a curious phenomenon that there never was a religion started in this world with more antagonism . . . [to the worship of forms] than Mohammedanism. . . . The Mohammedans can have neither painting, nor sculpture, nor music. . . . That would lead to formalism. The priest never faces his audience. If he did, that would make a distinction. This way there is none. And yet it was not two centuries after the Prophet's death before saint worship [developed]. Here is the toe of the saint! There is the skin of the saint! So it goes. Formal worship is one of the stages we have to pass through.

Therefore, instead of crusading against it, let us take the best in worship and study its underlying principles.

Of course, the lowest form of worship is what is known as [tree and stone worship]. Every crude, uncultured man will take up anything and add to it some idea [of his own]; and that will help him. He may worship a bit of bone, or stone — anything. In all these crude states of worship man has never worshipped a stone as stone, a tree as tree. You know that from common sense. Scholars sometimes say that men worshipped stones and trees. That is all nonsense. Tree worship is one of the stages through which the human race passed. Never, really, was there ever worship of anything but the spirit by man. He is spirit [and] can feel nothing but spirit. Divine mind could never make such a gross mistake as [to worship spirit as matter]. In this case, man conceived the stone as spirit or the tree as spirit. He [imagined] that some part of that Being resides in [the stone] or the tree, that [the stone or] the tree has a soul.

Tree worship and serpent worship always go together. There is the tree of knowledge. There must always be the tree, and the tree is somehow connected with the serpent. These are the oldest [forms of worship]. Even there you find that some particular tree or some particular stone is worshipped, not all the [trees or] stones in the world.

A higher state in [formal worship is that of] images [of ancestors and God]. People make images of men who have died and imaginary images of God. Then they worship those images.

Still higher is the worship of saints, of good men and women who have passed on. Men worship their relics. [They feel that] the presence of the saints is somehow in the relics, and that they will help them. [They believe that] if they touch the saint's bone, they will be healed — not that the bone itself heals, but that the saint who resides there does. . . .

These are all low states of worship and yet worship. We all have to pass through them. It is only from an intellectual standpoint that they are not good enough. In our hearts we cannot get rid of them. [If] you take from a man all the saints and images and do not allow him to go into a temple, [he will still] imagine all the gods. He has to. A man of eighty told me he could not conceive God except as an old man with a long beard sitting on a cloud. What does that show? His education is not complete. There has not been any spiritual education, and he is unable to conceive anything except in human terms.

There is still a higher order of formal worship — the world of symbolism. The forms are still there, but they are neither trees, nor [stones], nor images, nor relics of saints. They are symbols. There are all sorts [of symbols] all over the world. The circle is a great symbol of eternity. . . . There is the square; the well-known symbol of the cross; and two figures like S and Z crossing each other.

Some people take it into their heads to see nothing in symbols. . . . [Others want] all sorts of abracadabra. If you tell them plain, simple truths, they will not accept them. . . . Human nature being [what it is], the less they understand the better — the greater man [they think] you are. In all ages in every country such worshippers are deluded by certain diagrams and forms. Geometry was the greatest science of all. The vast majority of the people knew nothing [of it. They believed that if] the geometrist just drew a square and said abracadabra at the four corners, the whole world would begin to turn, the heavens would open, and God would come down and jump about and be a slave. There is a whole mass of lunatics today poring over these things day and night. All this is a sort of disease. It is not for the metaphysician at all; it is for the physician.

I am making fun, but I am so sorry. I see this problem so [grave] in India These are signs of the decay of the race, of degradation and duress. The sign of vigour, the sign of life, the sign of hope, the sign of health, the sign of everything that is good, is strength. As long as the body lives, there must be strength in the body, strength in the mind, [and strength] in the hand. In wanting to get spiritual power through [all this abracadabra] there is fear, fear of life. I do not mean that sort of symbolism.

But there is some truth in symbolistic. There cannot be any falsehood without some truth behind it. There cannot be any imitation without something real.

There is the symbolic form, of worship in the different religions. There are fresh, vigorous, poetic, healthy symbols Think of the marvellous power the symbol of the cross has had upon millions of people! Think of the symbol of the crescent! Think of the magnetism of this one symbol! Everywhere there are good and great symbols in the world. They interpret the spirit and bring [about] certain conditions of the mind; as a rule we find [they create] a tremendous power of faith and love.

Compare the Protestant with the Catholic [Church]. Who has produced more saints, more martyrs within the last four hundred years [during which] both have been in existence? The tremendous appeal of Catholic ceremonialism — all those lights, incense, candles, and the robes of the priests — has a great effect in itself. Protestantism is quite austere and unpoetic. The Protestants have gained many things, have granted a great deal more freedom in certain lines than the Catholics have, and so have a clear, more individualized conception. That is all right, but they have lost a good deal. . . . Take the paintings in the churches. That is an attempt at poetry. If we are hungry for poetry, why not have it? Why not give the soul what it wants? We have to have music. The Presbyterians were even against music. They are the "Mohammedans" of the Christians. Down with all poetry! Down with all ceremonials! Then they produce music. It appeals to the senses. I have seen how collectively they strive for the ray of light there over the pulpit.

Let the soul have its fill of poetry and religion represented on the external plane. Why not . . . ? You cannot fight [formal worship]. It will conquer again and again. . . . If you do not like what the Catholics do, do better. But we will neither do anything better nor have the poetry that already exists. That is a terrible state of things! Poetry is absolutely necessary. You may be the greatest philosopher in the world. But philosophy is the highest poetry. It is not dry bones It is essence of things. The Reality itself is more poetic than any dualism. . . .

Learning has no place in religion; for the majority learning is a block in the way. . . . A man my have read all the libraries in the world and many not be religious at all, and another, who cannot perhaps write his own name, senses religion and realises it. The whole of religion is our own inner perception. When I use the words "man-making religion", I do not mean books, nor dogmas, nor theories. I mean the man who has realised, has fully perceived, something of that infinite presence in his own heart.

The man at whose feet I sat all my life — and it is only a few ideas of his that try to teach — could [hardly] write his name at all. All my life I have not seen another man like that, and I have travelled all over the world. When I think of that man, I feel like a fool, because I want to read books and he never did. He never wanted to lick the plates after other people had eaten. That is why he was his own book. All my life I am repeating what Jack said and John said, and never say anything myself. What glory is it that you know what John said twenty-five years ago and what Jack said five years ago? Tell me what *you* have to say.

Mind you, there is no value in learning. You are all mistaken in learning. The only value of knowledge is in the strengthening, the disciplining, of the mind. By all this eternal swallowing it is a wonder that we are not all dyspeptics. Let us stop, and burn all the books, and get hold of ourselves and think. You all talk [about] and get distracted over losing your "individuality". You are losing it every moment of your lives by this eternal swallowing. If any one of you believes what I teach, I will be sorry. I will only be too glad if I can excite in you the power of thinking for yourselves. . . . My ambition is to talk to men and women, not to sheep. By men and women, I mean individuals. You are not little babies to drag all the filthy rags from the street and bind them up into a doll!

"This is a place for learning! That man is placed in the university! He knows all about what Mr. Blank said!" But Mr. Blank said nothing! If I had the choice I would . . . say to the professor, "Get out! You are nobody! " Remember this individualism at any cost! Think wrong if you will, no matter whether you get truth or not. The whole point is to discipline the mind. That truth which you swallow from others will not be yours. You cannot teach truth from my mouth; neither can you learn truth from my mouth. None can teach another. You have to realise truth and work it out for yourself according to your own nature. . . . All must struggle to be individuals — strong, standing on your own feet, thinking your own thoughts, realising your own Self. No use swallowing doctrines others pass on — standing up together like soldiers in jail, sitting down together, all eating the same food, all nodding their heads at the same time. Variation is the sign of life. Sameness is the sign of death.

Once I was in an Indian city, and an old man came to me. He said, "Swami, teach me the way." I saw that that man was as dead as this table before me. Mentally and spiritually he was really dead. I said, "will you do what I ask you to do? Can you steal? Can you drink wine? Can you eat meat?"

The man [exclaimed], "What are you teaching!"

I said to him, "Did this wall ever steal? Did the wall ever drink wine?"

"No, sir."

Man steals, and he drinks wine, and becomes God. "I know you are not the wall, my friend. Do something! Do something! " I saw that if that man stole, his soul would be on the way to salvation.

How do I know that you are individuals — all saying the same thing, all standing up and sitting down together? That is the road to death! Do something for your souls! Do wrong if you please, but do something! You will understand me by and by, if you do not just now. Old age has come upon the soul, as it were. It has become rusty. The rust must be [rubbed off], and then we go on. Now you understand why there is evil in the world. Go home and think of that, just to take off that rustiness!

We pray for material things. To attain some end we worship God with shopkeeping worship. Go on and pray for food and clothes! Worship is good. Something is always better than nothing. "A blind uncle is better than no uncle at all." A very rich young man becomes ill, and then to get rid of his disease he begins to give to the poor. That is good, but it is not religion yet, not spiritual religion. It is all on the material plane. What is material, and what is not? When the world is the end and God the means to attain that end, that is material. When God is the end and the world is only the means to attain that end, spirituality has begun.

Thus, to the man who wants this [material] life enough, all his heavens are a continuance of this life. He wants to see all the people who are dead, and have a good time once more.

There was one of those ladies who bring the departed spirits down to us — a medium. She was very large, yet she was called medium. Very good! This lady liked me very much and invited me to come. The spirits were all very polite to me. I had a very peculiar experience. You understand, it was a [seance], midnight. The medium said, ". . . I see a ghost standing here. The ghost tells me that there is a Hindu gentleman on that bench." I stood up and said, "It required no ghost to tell you that."

There was a young man present who was married, intelligent, and well educated. He was there to see his mother. The medium said, "So-and-so's mother is here." This young man had been telling me about his mother. She was very thin when she died, but the mother that came out of the screen! You ought to have seen her! I wanted to see what this young man would do. To my surprise he jumped up and embraced this spirit and said. "Oh mother, how beautiful you have grown in the spirit land!" I said, "I am blessed that I am here. It gives me an insight into human nature!"

Going back to our formal worship. . . . it is a low state of worship when you worship God as a means to the end, which is this life and this world. . . . The vast majority of [people] have never had any conception of anything higher than this lump of flesh and the joys of the senses. Even in this life, all the pleasures these poor souls have are the same as the beasts. . . . They eat animals. They love their children. Is that all the glory of man? And we worship God Almighty! What for? Just to give us these material things and defend them all the time. . . . It means we have not gone beyond the [animals and] birds. We are no better. We do not know any better. And woe unto us, we should know better! The only difference is that they do not have a God like ours. . . We have the same five senses [as the animals], only theirs are better. We cannot eat a morsel of food with the relish that a dog chews a bone. They have more pleasure in life than we; so we are a little less than animals.

Why should you want to be something that any power in nature can operate better? This is the most important question for you to think about. What do you want — this life, these senses, this body, or something infinitely higher and better, something from which there is no more fall, no more change?

So what does it mean . . . ? You say, "Lord, give me my bread, my money! Heal my diseases! Do this and that!" Every time you say that, you are hypnotising yourselves with the idea, "I am matter, and this matter is the goal." Every time you try to fulfil a material desire, you tell yourselves that you are [the] body, that you are not spirit. . . .

Thank God, this is a dream! Thank God, for it will vanish! Thank God, there is death, glorious death, because it ends all this delusion, this dream, this fleshiness, this anguish. No dream can be eternal; it must end sooner or later. There is none who can keep his dream for ever. I thank God that it is so! Yet this form of worship is all right. Go on! To pray for something is better than nothing. These are the stages through which we pass. These are the first lessons. Gradually, the mind begins to think of something higher than the senses, the body, the enjoyments of this world.

How does [man] do it? First he becomes a thinker. When you think upon a problem, there is no sense enjoyment there, but [the] exquisite delight of thought. . . . It is that that makes the man. . . . Take one great idea! It deepens. Concentration comes. You no longer feel your body. Your senses have stopped. You are above all physical senses. All that was manifesting itself through the senses is concentrated upon that one idea. That moment you are higher than the animal. You get the revelation none can take from you — a direct perception of something higher than the body. . . . Therein is the gold of mind, not upon the plane of the senses.

Thus, working through the plane of the senses, you get more and more entry into the other regions, and then this world falls away from you. You get one glimpse of that spirit, and then your senses and your sense-enjoyments, your dinging to the flesh, will all melt away from you. Glimpse after glimpse will come from the realm of spirit. You will have finished Yoga, and spirit will stand revealed as spirit. Then you will begin the worship of God as spirit. Then you will begin to understand that worship is not to gain something. At heart, our worship was that infinite-finite element, love, which [is] an eternal sacrifice at the feet of the Lord by the soul. "Thou and not I. I am dead. Thou art, and I am not. I do not want wealth nor beauty, no, nor even learning. I do not want salvation. If it be Thy will, let me go into twenty million hells. I only want one thing: Be Thou my love!"

(Vedanta and the West, Nov.-Dec. 1955)

Divine Love

(This lecture is reproduced from the
Vedanta and the West. See Vol. IV.)

(Delivered in San Francisco area, April 12, 1900)

[Love may be symbolised by a triangle. The first angle is,] love questions not. It is not a beggar. . . . Beggar's love is no love at all. The first sign of love is when love asks nothing, [when it] gives everything. This is the real spiritual worship, the worship through love. Whether God is merciful is no longer questioned. He is God; He is my love. Whether God is omnipotent and almighty, limited or unlimited, is no longer questioned. If He distributes good, all right; if He brings evil, what does it matter? All other attributes vanish except that one — infinite love.

There was an old Indian emperor who on a hunting expedition came across a great sage in the forest. He was so pleased with this sage that he insisted that the latter come to the capital to receive some presents. [At first] the sage refused. [But] the emperor insisted, and at last the sage consented. When he arrived [at the palace], he was announced to the emperor who said, "Wait a minute until I finish my prayer." The emperor prayed, "Lord, give me more wealth, more [land, more health], more children." The sage stood up and began to walk out of the room. The emperor said, "You have not received my presents." The sage replied, "I do not beg from beggars. All this time you have been praying for more land, [for] more money, for this and that. What can you give me? First satisfy your own wants!"

Love never asks; it always gives. . . . When a young man goes to see his sweetheart, . . . there is no business relationship between them; theirs is a relationship of love, and love is no beggar. [In the same way], we understand that the beginning of real spiritual worship means no begging. We have finished all begging: "Lord, give me this and that." Then will religion begin.

The second [angle of the triangle of love] is that love knows no fear. You may cut me to pieces, and I [will] still love you. Suppose one of you mothers, a weak woman, sees a tiger in the street snatching your child. I know where you will be: you will face the tiger. Another time a dog appears in the street, and you will fly. But you jump at the mouth of the tiger and snatch your child away. Love knows no fear. It conquers all evil. The fear of

God is the beginning of religion, but the love of God is the end of religion. All fear has died out.

The third [angle of the love-triangle is that] love is its own end. It can never be the means. The man who says, "I love you for such and such a thing", does not love. Love can never be the means; it must be the perfect end. What is the end and aim of love? To love God, that is all. Why should one love God? [There is] no why, because it is not the means. When one can love, that is salvation, that is perfection, that is heaven. What more? What else can be the end? What can you have higher than love?

I am not talking about what every one of us means by love. Little namby-pamby love is lovely. Man rails in love with woman, and woman goes to die for man. The chances are that in five minutes John kicks Jane, and Jane kicks John. This is a materialism and no love at all. If John could really love Jane, he would be perfect that moment. [His true] nature is love; he is perfect in himself. John will get all the powers of Yoga simply by loving Jane, [although] he may not know a word about religion, psychology, or theology. I believe that if a man and woman can really love, [they can acquire] all the powers the Yogis claim to have, for love itself is God. That God is omnipresent, and [therefore] you have that love, whether you know it or not.

I saw a boy waiting for a girl the other evening. . . . I thought it a good experiment to study this boy. He developed clairvoyance and clairaudience through the intensity of his love. Sixty or seventy times he never made a mistake, and the girl was two hundred miles away. [He would say], "She is dressed this way." [Or], "There she goes." I have seen that with my own eyes.

This is the question: Is not your husband God, your child God? If you can love your wife, you have all the religion in the world. You have the whole secret of religion and Yoga in you. But can you love? That is the question. You say, "I love . . . Oh Mary, I die for you! " [But if you] see Mary kissing another man, you want to cut his throat. If Mary sees John talking to another girl, she cannot sleep at night, and she makes life hell for John. This is not love. This is barter and sale in sex. It is blasphemy to talk of it as love. The world talks day and night of God and religion — so of love. Making a sham of everything, that is what you are doing! Everybody talks of love, [yet in the] columns in the newspapers [we read] of divorces every day. When you love John, do you love John for his sake or for your sake? [If you love him for your sake], you expect something from John. [If you love him for his sake], you do not want anything from John. He can do anything he likes, [and] you [will] love him just the same.

These are the three points, the three angles that constitute the triangle [of love]. Unless there is love, philosophy becomes dry bones, psychology becomes a sort of [theory], and work becomes mere labour. [If there is love], philosophy becomes poetry, psychology becomes [mysticism], and work the most delicious thing in creation. [By merely] reading books [one] becomes barren. Who becomes learned? He who can feel even one drop of love. God is love, and love is God. And God is everywhere. After seeing that God is love and God is everywhere, one does not know whether one stands on one's head or [on one's] feet — like a man who gets a bottle of wine and does not know where he stands. . . . If we weep ten minutes for God, we will not know where we are for the next two months. . . . We will not remember the times for meals. We will not know what we are eating. [How can] you love God and always be so nice and businesslike? . . . The . . . all-conquering, omnipotent power of love — how can it come? . . .

Judge people not. They are all mad. Children are [mad] after their games, the young after the young, the old [are] chewing the cud of their past years; some are mad after gold. Why not some after God? Go crazy over the love of God as you go crazy over Johns and Janes. Who are they? [people] say, "Shall I give up this? Shall I give up that?" One asked, "Shall I give up marriage?" Do not give up anything! Things will give you up. Wait, and you will forget them.

[To be completely] turned into love of God — there is the real worship! You have a glimpse of that now and then in the Roman Catholic Church — some of those wonderful monks and nuns going mad with marvellous love. Such love you ought to have! Such should be the love of God — without asking anything, without seeking anything. . . .

The question was asked: How to worship? Worship Him as dearer than all your possessions, dearer than all your relatives, [dearer than] your children. [Worship Him as] the one you love as Love itself. There is one whose name is infinite Love. That is the only definition of God. Do not care if this . . . universe is destroyed. What do we care as long as He is infinite love? [Do you see what worship means? All other thoughts must go. Everything must vanish except God. The love the father or mother has for the child, [the love] the wife [has] for the husband, the husband, for the wife, the friend for the friend — all these loves concentrated into one must be given to God. Now, if the woman loves the man, she cannot love another man. If the man loves the woman, he cannot love another [woman]. Such is the nature of love.

My old Master used to say, "Suppose there is a bag of gold in this room, and in the next room there is a robber. The robber is well aware that there is a bag of gold. Would the robber be able to sleep? Certainly not. All the time he would be crazy thinking how to reach the gold." . . . [Similarly], if a man loves God, how can he love anything else? How can anything else stand before that mighty love of God? Everything else vanishes [before it]. How can the mind stop without going crazy to find [that love], to realise, to feel, to live in that?

This is how we are to love God: "I do not want wealth, nor [friends, nor beauty], nor possessions, nor learning, nor even salvation. If it be Thy will, send me a thousand deaths. Grant me, this — that I may love Thee and that for love's sake. That love which materialistic persons have for their worldly possessions, may that strong love come into my heart, but only for the Beautiful. Praise to God! Praise to God the Lover!" God is nothing else than that. He does not care for the wonderful things many Yogis can do. Little magicians do little tricks. God is the big magician; He does all the tricks. Who cares how many worlds [there are]? . . .

There is another [way. It is to] conquer everything, [to] subdue everything — to conquer the body [and] the mind. . . . "What is the use of conquering everything? My business is with God! " [says the devotee.]

There was one Yogi, a great lover. He was dying of cancer of the throat. He [was] visited [by] another Yogi, who was a philosopher. [The latter] said, "Look here, my friend, why don't you concentrate your mind on that sore of yours and get it cured?" The third time this question was asked [this great Yogi] said, "Do you think it possible that the [mind] which I have given entirely to the Lord [can be fixed upon this cage of flesh and blood]?" Christ refused to bring legions of angels to his aid. Is this little body so great that I should bring twenty thousand angels to keep it two or three days more?

[From the worldly standpoint,] my all is this body. My world is this body. My God is this body. I am the body. If you pinch me, I am pinched. I forget God the moment I have a headache. I am the body! God and everything must come down for this highest goal — the body. From this standpoint, when Christ died on the cross and did not bring angels [to his aid], he was a fool. He ought to have brought down angels and gotten himself off the cross! But from the standpoint of the lover, to whom this body is nothing, who cares for this nonsense? Why bother thinking about this body that comes and goes? There is no more to it than the piece of cloth the Roman soldiers cast lots for.

There is a whole gamut of difference between [the worldly standpoint] and the lover's standpoint. Go on loving. If a man is angry, there is no reason why you should be angry; if he degrades himself, that is no reason why you should degrade yourself. . . . "Why should I become angry just because another man has made a fool of himself. Do thou resist not evil!" That is what the lovers of God say. Whatever the world does, wherever it goes, has no influence [on them].

One Yogi had attained supernatural powers. He said, "See my power! See the sky; I will cover it with clouds." It began to rain. [Someone] said, "My lord, you are wonderful. But teach me that, knowing which, I shall not ask for anything else." ... To get rid even of power, to have nothing, not to want power! [What this means] cannot be understood simply by intellect. . . . You cannot understand by reading thousands of books. ... When we begin to understand, the whole world opens before us. ... The girl is playing with her dolls, getting new husbands all the time; but when her real husband comes, all the dolls will be put away [for ever]. ... So [with] all these goings-on here. [When] the sun of love rises, all these play-suns of power and these [cravings] all pass [away]. What shall we do with power? Thank God if you can get rid of the power that you have. Begin to love. Power must go. Nothing must stand between me and God except love. God is only love and nothing else — love first, love in the middle, and love at the end.

[There is the] story of a queen preaching [the love of God] in the streets. Her enraged husband persecuted her, and she was hunted up and down the country. She used to sing songs describing her [love]. Her songs have been sung everywhere. "With tears in my eyes I [nourished the everlasting creeper] of love. ..." This is the last, the great [goal]. What else is there? [People] want this and that. They all want to have and possess. That is why so few understand [love], so few come to it. Wake them and tell them! They will get a few more hints.

Love itself is the eternal, endless sacrifice. You will have to give up everything. You cannot take possession of anything. Finding love, you will never [want] anything [else]. ... "Only be Thou my love for ever! " That is what love wants. "My love, one kiss of those lips! [For him] who has been kissed by Thee, all sorrows vanish. Once kissed by Thee, man becomes happy and forgets love of everything else. He praises Thee alone and he sees Thee alone." In the nature of human love even, [there lurk divine elements. In] the first moment of intense love the whole world seems in tune with your own heart. Every bird in the universe sings your love; the flowers bloom for you. It is infinite, eternal love itself that [human] love comes from.

Why should the lover of God fear anything — fear robbers, fear distress, fear even for his life? ... The lover [may]go to the utmost hell, but would it be hell? We all have to give up these ideas of heaven [and hell] and get greater [love]. ... Hundreds there are seeking this madness of love before which everything [but God vanishes].

At last, love, lover, and beloved become one. That is the goal. ... Why is there any separation between soul and man, between soul and God? . . . Just to have this enjoyment of love. He wanted to love Himself, so He split Himself into many . . . "This is the whole reason for creation", says the lover. "We are all one. 'I and my Father are one.' Just now I am separate in order to love God. ... Which is better — to become sugar or to eat sugar? To become sugar, what fun is that:? To eat sugar — that is infinite enjoyment of love."

All the ideals of love — [God] as [our] father, mother, friend, child — [are conceived in order to strengthen devotion in us and make us feel nearer and dearer to God]. The intensest love is that between the sexes. God must be loved with that sort of love The woman loves her father; she loves her mothers she loves her child; she loves her friend. But she cannot express herself all to the father, nor to the mother, nor to the child, nor to the friend. There is only one person from whom she does not hide anything. So with the man. ... The [husband-] wife relationship is the all-rounded relationship. The relationship of the sexes [has] all the other loves concentrated into one. In the husband, the woman has the father, the friend, the child. In the wife, the husband has mother, daughter, and something else. That tremendous complete love of the sexes must come [for God] — that same love with which a woman opens herself to a man without any bond of blood — perfectly, fearlessly, and shamelessly. No darkness! She would no more hide anything from her lover than she would from her own self. That very love must come [for God]. These things are hard and difficult to understand. You will begin to understand by and by, and all idea of sex will fall away. "Like the water drop on the sand of the river bank on a summer day, even so is this life and all its relations."

All these ideas [like] "He is the creator", are ideas fit for children. He is my love, my life itself — that must be the cry of my heart! ...

"I have one hope. They call Thee the Lord of the world, and — good or evil, great or small — I am part of the world, and Thou art also my love. My body, my mind, and my soul are all at Thy altar. Love, refuse these gifts not!"

(Vedanta and the West, Sept.-Oct. 1955)

* 9 7 8 9 3 5 9 3 9 3 6 8 1 *